# A BROADS-EYE VIEW

## THE NORFOLK BROADS THROUGH AERIAL PHOTOGRAPHY

MIKE PAGE

HALSGROVE

First published in Great Britain in 2005
Reprinted 2005, 2007

Copyright © 2005 photographs Mike Page
Copyright © 2005 text Pauline Young

**British Library Cataloguing-in-Publication Data**
A CIP record for this title is available from the British Library

ISBN 978 1 84114 447 4

**HALSGROVE**
Halsgrove House
Lower Moor Way
Tiverton, Devon EX16 6SS
Tel: 01884 243242
Fax: 01884 243325
email: sales@halsgrove.com
website: www.halsgrove.com

Printed and bound by D'Auria Industrie Grafiche Spa, Italy

# CONTENTS

# ACKNOWLEDGEMENTS

We'd like to thank the many expert individuals and organizations who have helped with the information contained in this book including The Broads Authority, the RSPB, The Museum of The Broads, Norfolk Record Office, Dr Martin George, Ray Allard, Brian Coleman, Elizabeth Ellis-Paul, James Hoseason, Patrick Lee, Keith Nunn, Jackie Routledge, Karen Sayer and particularly Roy Snelling who made it all possible

Thanks also to Norwich Air Traffic for their flight information service and the many co-pilots from Seething Airfield.

Also to our respective spouses Gillian and John for whose continuing patience and good humour throughout the production we are grateful.

Mike Page, Strumpshaw
Pauline Young, Norwich
March 2005

# FOREWORD

I first met Mike Page around 40 years ago when he was dedicated to repairing my dead or dented van and I was repairing television receivers. Neither vehicles nor televisions were as reliable as they are today and much ingenuity was required to achieve a fast dependable repair. Mike's enthusiasm in those days was outstanding and a telephone call for help always met with an immediate response.

Here was Mike 40 years later, in my office saying 'Roy, I need your help'. My brain did a rapid recall to those early days and I had no hesitation in offering this without any reservations. 'I have made a video of the East Anglian Coast and would like you to market it'. Knowing Mike's dedication to anything he undertook and his desire for perfection, I was happy to do so.

He continued 'we could sell it for charity'. With a commitment like that I couldn't refuse, and helped in any way I could. All profits went to charity and we both got a tremendous thrill as the number of videos sold increased.

This book is a continuation of the video, with a collection of superb aerial photographs. I am sure it will be treasured by all of us who live here, and all who have visited. Broadland is such a beautiful place and and yet many of us who have lived in East Anglia all our lives will not have seen some of the sites shown here as they are inaccessible on foot or by boat. Pauline Young's text has added helpful descriptions.

I am sure this book will find its way onto the bookshelves of lovers of Broadland all over the world.

**Roy Snelling**
**Blofield Heath, Norfolk, March 2005**

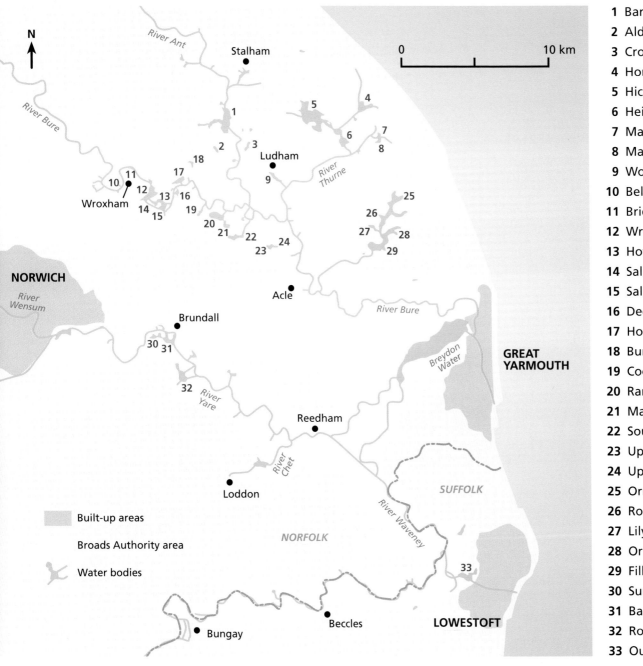

N

Stalham

0          10 km

1 Barton Broad
2 Alderfen Broad
3 Crome's Broad
4 Horsey Mere
5 Hickling Broad
6 Heigham Sound
7 Martham North
8 Martham South
9 Womack Water
10 Belaugh Broad
11 Bridge Broad
12 Wroxham Broad
13 Hoveton Great Broad
14 Salhouse Little Broad
15 Salhouse Broad
16 Decoy Broad
17 Hoveton Little Broad
18 Burnt Fen Broad
19 Cockshoot Broad
20 Ranworth Broad
21 Malthouse Broad
22 South Walsham Broad
23 Upton Great Broad
24 Upton Little Broad
25 Ormesby Broad
26 Rollesby Broad
27 Lily Broad
28 Ormesby Little Broad
29 Filby Broad
30 Surlingham Broad
31 Bargate Broad
32 Rockland Broad
33 Oulton Broad

River Ant

River Bure

NORWICH

River Wensum

Ludham

River Thurne

Wroxham

Acle

Brundall

River Bure

GREAT YARMOUTH

Breydon Water

Reedham

River Yare

River Chet

Loddon

SUFFOLK

River Waveney

NORFOLK

Beccles

LOWESTOFT

Bungay

Built-up areas

Broads Authority area

Water bodies

# INTRODUCTION

Since I learned to fly over forty years ago I have been fortunate in being able to combine aviation with my other consuming interest, photography. My present camera is a Canon 1D Mk2 8.5 megapixel Digital with a 2 GB memory card. Canon 24-70 f2.8 L and Canon 80-200 f2.8 L lenses, both with UV filters, give me the ideal combination for all aerial photography. I use shutter priority settings with shutter speeds of 1/150 second to 1/1000 second, allowing me to photograph in all conditions including turbulence. From the air an entirely different perspective presents itself. Mist over marshes, reed beds in winter, sailing boats tacking across a Broadland river, when all viewed from a thousand feet or so look entirely different, and I hope I have managed to communicate this fascination in my pictures.

The coastline was my particular passion in my early days of aerial photography. As a young boy I lived in Beccles and used to go beach fishing at Covehithe and Benacre. This part of the shoreline has been disappearing rapidly and I decided to capture an 'historical' record of erosion along the coastline and store these pictures as part of a photographic library. My 35mm film collection now comprises some 25 000 pictures recording many changes throughout East Anglia. Towns, villages, major developments, coastal erosion and far reaching views of Norfolk and Suffolk all are stored in my library, available to everyone as an archive. Latterly digital photography has enabled me to store whichever images I choose, without the need for expensive processing, and to date I have around 6000 digital files on my computer.

My camera is hand held whilst photographing from the aircraft, thus the need to sometimes use fast shutter speeds to counteract the turbulence. The ideal aircraft is a Cessna 150 which I fly with the window permanently latched open to avoid distortion through the glass. Always I have another pilot to handle the aircraft and keep a lookout whilst I'm taking pictures.

Through this and other planned books I hope to give everyone the chance to enjoy some of the exciting and interesting views of East Anglia I have been privileged to see. My thanks go to Pauline Young for the explanatory captions.

All royalties from the sales of this and subsequent books I intend to donate to charity.

**Mike Page**
**Strumpshaw, Norfolk, May 2005**

# The Character of Broadland

Aerial photographs add a dimension to our understanding of an area. This particular picture, encompassing the area around the Ant, Bure and Thurne, was taken from an altitude of 6000 feet and shows many of the aspects which make up the very special area we call The Broads. River crossings, broads, archaeological sites, marshes, river diversions, boatyards, dykes, reed beds and wind-pump restorations, all can be spotted within this picture.

Ludham Bridge (bottom left) crosses the River Ant about a mile from its mouth at the River Bure. A ford crossed here originally, as was the case at many Broads' crossings. The bridge replaced an earlier one in the 1920s. St Benet's Abbey (bottom centre) has stood here since the eleventh century, the fishponds standing out as rectangles north of the ruined gatehouse. Ward Marsh (bottom of picture) is bounded by the original course of the Bure. Many rivers were straightened to enable faster passage of trading boats, particularly the wherry. Fleet Dyke (east side of Ward Marsh) leads to South Walsham Broad.

The Hundred Dyke was the original course of the Ant into the Thurne. It shows as a wavy line just south of Ludham Bridge, meandering across marshland to join the Thurne upriver of Thurne Drainage Mill.

Thurne Mouth is at the acute angle of the Bure (centre right). The Thurne originally flowed northwards into the sea north of Horsey. Below Thurne Dyke on the opposite bank is St Benet's Level drainage Mill, restored in 2001. Womack Water (mid picture) contains the premises housing historic boats: the Hunter Fleet of traditional wooden sailing boats is here, and wherry *Albion*'s winter base is almost next door. Herbert Woods' boatyard (now the Funnel Group) is at Potter Heigham near the medieval bridge (top centre). The Thurne flows to Martham Broad (top centre) with a dyke off through Heigham Sound to Hickling Broad and Horsey Mere. Although the wind turbines at Somerton are not strictly in Broadland they dominate parts of the skyline and are part of the backdrop of the Trinity Broads (right top of picture).

The proximity of the coastline demonstrates The Broads' vulnerability to invasion by the sea – as has happened several times over the centuries.

# THE BURE

With over 48 kilometres of navigable waterway the River Bure, also known as the 'North River', is the longest of all Broadland rivers. It rises near Melton Constable and was canalised between Aylsham and Coltishall, although the Aylsham Navigation is no longer navigable.

## Coltishall

*Ella*, the last trading wherry, was built here at Allen's Yard in 1912. The end of navigation is hidden in the trees (top left) although remains of the first lock (last used in 1912) on the Aylsham Navigation is visible from the river and used as a sluice for flood control. There are two pubs in the group of buildings on the river mid picture, the Rising Sun (closest to the river) and the Kings Head. The first Roys store was opened in Coltishall in 1895. Roys of Wroxham (actually in Hoveton) later achieved fame with the claim that theirs was 'the largest village store in the world'.

## Belaugh

The church stands high (high for Norfolk) and is Norman in origin. A steep path from the river and through the churchyard leads to the church, a favourite of John Betjeman. Nearby is a private dyke leading to an area known as 'Little Switzerland' where marl was once dug.

## Wroxham

The Boat hire industry began at Wroxham when, towards the end of the nineteenth century, John Loynes rented out boats from his yard near Wroxham Bridge. Wroxham's claim to be the 'Capital of The Broads' is justified on a busy day in the summe, but the River Bure flows through noticeably more rural surroundings upstream of Wroxham Bridge. Bridge Broad (mid picture right) has been open to navigation only since the 1970s and has a 'closed in' feel with trees growing right at the water's edge. Wroxham church (top picture between the railway line and the river) stands a considerable distance from what is now, since the advent of the holiday industry, considered to be the village centre. Belaugh Broad (top) was part of a 1987 project to clear phosphate-laden water by suction-pumping mud on to adjacent land to encourage new plant growth.

## Wroxham and Hoveton – looking upstream

The new footbridge across the Bure at last separates vehicles and pedestrians. Broads Tours premises are centre picture with a line of day boats to the right. The river separates the parishes of Wroxham (left of picture) and Hoveton. Roys of Wroxham (actually in Hoveton but the alliteration better slips off the tongue!), occupies all four corners at the crossroads (top right).

## Wroxham Broad

Wroxham Broad (near picture) with its two entrances is separated from the river by a very narrow strip of carr (water-tolerant) vegetation. Teams have been clearing the trees away in the hope that reed swamp with grow again and provide a wider separation. Hoveton Great Broad (mid picture right) lies opposite Salhouse Broad, with Decoy Broad mid picture and Hoveton Little Broad (Black Horse Broad) almost opposite. Horning village is strung along the river in the distance, with Ranworth Broad top right.

## Hoveton Great Broad

Accessible only by boat there's a signed boardwalk around part of the broad where, from a hide during the nesting season, terns can be seen congregating on specially built rafts. Salhouse Broad is on the left, and Wroxham Broad in the background.

## Hoveton Great Broad – Fish Barrier

The circular structures are intended to protect water lilies from being grazed by coot and other waterfowl, a fish barrier surrounds two of them. This was part of an experiment to try to obtain clearer water; the fish were eating smaller creatures such as water fleas which are part of a complicated chain which helps combat turbidity caused by nutrient-rich run-off from the land. The darker area inside the enclosure reveals the relatively clearer water.

## Hoveton Little Broad

In 1949 Herbert Woods successfully led a campaign to reopen Hoveton Little Broad (top centre), also known as Black Horse Broad, as part of a movement to restore full navigation rights over all broads and rivers. A barrier had been placed by the landowner across Black Horse Dyke. Herbert Woods was among the group of the men who winched up the tree trunks from the dyke entrance. That night in the Black Horse pub drinks were on the house. The broad is open to the public from Easter to September.

## Horning Village

Horning is 'Coot Club' country. Horning Sailing Club (centre picture) founded the 'Three Rivers Race' when new young committee member David Hastings was asked to think of an activity which would create some interest within the sailing community. The race takes place annually in early June and takes between 11 and 18 hours depending on the wind and tide. The three rivers are the Bure, Ant and Thurne. Opposite (top right) are Woodbastwick marshes.

## Horning

Horning Town Reach and Lower Street from the opposite direction. Wherry *Hathor* (bottom picture) being sailed and quanted across the river.

## Ranworth and Malthouse Broads

The two broads are linked by a narrow channel through which a ferry runs to the Norfolk Wildlife Trust's floating Information Centre on Ranworth (the farther broad). Where once wherries would have tied up to offload barley for the malthouse, holiday cruisers now compete for a mooring. It's permitted (even encouraged!) to climb the tower of St Helen's church (centre left) to get a view almost as good as this one.

## Fleet Dyke leading to South Walsham *Above*

The original route of the river to South Walsham Broad was the large loop of Ward Marsh but, as with much of Broadland, man intervened and straightened the river so that trading boats (the wherries and their forerunners) had quicker passage.

## The Stew Ponds *Right*

The rectangular ponds near the ruins of St Benet's Abbey Gatehouse are the remains of a larger area where fish were held to provide the monks with food. The inner and outer areas of South Walsham Broad are in the distance and are fed from the Fleet Dyke.

## South Walsham Broad

The inner half of South Walsham Broad leads to the Fairhaven Water Gardens; craft are permitted there but not allowed to moor.

## St Benet's Abbey

A Benedictine abbey (dedicated to St Benet or Benedict) has been sited here since before the Norman Conquest. The remains are now principally outlines of buildings and earthworks on what was an extensive site. The foreground rectangles were fish ponds (stew ponds), and nearby was a swan pit for fattening cygnets for the table. Between the river and the gatehouse was a horse pond and stables, and a dock may have been sited where the reed now grows. The wooden cross (mid field) came from oak from the Sandringham Estate and was erected in 1987 on the site of the original church. Each August the Bishop of Norwich (who is also the Abbot of St Benet's) conducts a service here. He generally arrives by wherry. Considerable bank erosion has taken place over the years: witness the outlines of buildings now at the water's edge.

## St Benet's Gatehouse

Among the Gatehouse ruins this mill for grinding colza seed for lamp oil was built in the eighteenth century. In the area of reeds to the left of the Gatehouse a dock was once situated and it may be possible to pick out the beginning of the causeway, just inland from it, linking St Benet's with St James' Hospital at Horning, crossing the River Ant via a wooden bridge.

## Acle Wey Bridge

This latest bridge is at least the third to be built here, and before that there was a ford. The road across the marshes between Acle and Great Yarmouth (the Acle Straight) wasn't made until the 1830s. Its name comes from the old English 'waeg' (a road), as also in 'Wayford' Bridge where also there had originally been a ford. This picture shows the almost completed new bridge in October 1997, with the temporary Bailey bridge about to be dismantled.

## The Trinity Broads

The Trinity Broads, in true Norfolk 'do different' style, actually number five (from the top of picture, Ormesby, Rollesby, Ormesby Little, Lily and Filby Broads). They are an expanse of landlocked water, those south of Ormesby Broad being made available only to a number of educational organisations for sailing and related sports. Ormesby Broad provides the water supply for Great Yarmouth. At one time these broads were connected to the Bure by the Muck Fleet, now a dammed-off stream and not navigable. The area surrounding the Trinity Broads was the slightly higher ground of the island of Flegg (a Norse word for reeds) Within Flegg there is a mile long causeway to Acle Wey Bridge.

## Stokesby
The pub (centre picture) takes its name from the ferry which used to cross the river here.

**Stracey Arms Mill on the River Bure** *Above and overleaf*
The mill, built in 1883, is open to the public. It and the pub nearby took their name from local landowner Sir Edward Stracey. The pub, originally a wherrymen's hostelry, has changed its name recently. The A47 'Acle Straight' road is an accident black-spot, the subject of much controversy as to how best to improve it. The land between the road and the Yarmouth-to-Norwich railway line is part of Halvergate marshes which stretch across to Breydon Water. The Broads Society have indicated that if eventually it is decided to dual the Acle Straight then the land between the railway line and the road should be a reed bed, thus offsetting ecological damage the road may cause. Great Yarmouth is on the skyline.

**Stracey Arms Mill**

## The Bure Loop

A recent bold plan to designate and change part of the area between the south bank of the Bure and Breydon Water into a new broad, and create both flood alleviation and leisure/wildlife areas, came to nothing on grounds of cost. At one time the Bure flowed not into the Yare below Breydon Bridge (centre), as it does today, but into the sea north of Caister (left).

# THE ANT

The Ant rises in Antingham Ponds near North Walsham and joins the Bure a mile below Ludham Bridge. It takes its name from Anta, an invading Norseman who made his ham (homestead) here. It is the shortest of the main rivers but the one whose course has been most altered. It is approximately six miles from the start of navigation at Horning Lock on the Dilham and North Walsham Canal to its mouth a mile below Ludham Bridge. Originally it emptied not into the Bure near St Benet's, but flowed along the Hundred Dyke (now only a ditch) into the Thurne upriver of Thurne Mill.

## Wayford Bridge

The A1151 Norwich-to-Great Yarmouth road, via Wroxham, crosses the river at Wayford Bridge where originally there was a ford. Upstream (near picture) the river was canalised and, in 1826, the Dilham and North Walsham Canal was opened. The boats were 'market wherries' or 'cabbage wherries', smaller than the average and able to pass under Wayford Bridge. The boats took market-garden produce as far as Great Yarmouth.

## The Ant, Stalham and Sutton Broad *Above*

Sutton Broad, the elongated stretch of water (right), leads to Sutton Staithe on the straight stretch of the A149, originally the M&GN railway line. Every Broadland village with water access has a staithe, (steath – a landing place). Much of the original area of the broad has silted up in the last two hundred years. The curious little island triangle between the broad and the left channel to Stalham (top left) is similar to the one at the north end of Barton Broad. The main river flows past Hunsett Mill (centre left) which is one of the most picturesque and photographed of the Broadland drainage mills.

## Hunsett Mill *Opposite*

This is thought to take its name from an eel sett owned by a man named Hunn.

## Stalham

This compact market town has one main street in which the church stands. It's now bypassed by the A149. The staithe was originally the main line of communication from the town.

## Stalham Staithe

Also known as the Poor's Staithe, this collection of buildings was once the hub of commercial traffic. The three-storeyed building (centre) is a former granary, and the centre complex, including a Victorian storage building, now houses the Museum of The Broads. Wherry, *Maud*, recently restored, is tied up alongside. The curious vessel on the end of the line of craft is a replica tug. The large buildings (centre) are the premises of a boatbuilder.

## Barton Broad looking north

'Pleasure Hill' is the small island to the right in the broad. Before its restoration as part of the Clearwater 2000 project it had almost disappeared. It had been a venue for many Victorian outings and picnics. Pleasure Hill is the remains of a causeway across the broad which separated the peat diggings of two parishes. The floating T shape near the channel leading to Neatishead is 'The Ark' and belongs to the Nancy Oldfield Trust which provides sailing and other Broads-related experiences to the disabled. At the far end of the broad the two channels leave a triangle of marsh known curiously as 'The Heater', a name of unknown origin. The left channel goes to Barton Turf, the right to Stalham and Wayford Bridge. The marked areas on the broad's fringe (near left) are also part of the Clearwater 2000 project.

## Clearwater 2000 *Above and right*

The Clearwater 2000 project began in 1995 with the aim of restoring a murky broad to the clarity it had before the Second World War. The broad was suction-dredged and the spoil placed on the adjacent land in lagoons. This photograph was taken in 1999 and the spoil has since been ploughed in. Fish were removed from the edge of the area known as Turkey Broad and kept out with a 'curtain'. Fish eat copious quantities of water fleas which are needed to keep the water clear and healthy, allowing water plants re-establish. The left-hand circle shows fourteen thousand purpose-made 'brushes' suspended in the water to provide structures for beneficial zooplankton, including water fleas, which eat up toxic algae. The fish barrier or curtain can be seen as the continuous line. A buoyed rope outside it has been installed to prevent damage from boats. The green circle is a temporary algal bloom formed because the water was both stagnant and nutrient rich. Two tern nesting-rafts are moored between the circles, installed by the Norfolk Wildlife Trust who have owned the broad since 1946. The whole project cost £3m and was funded by the Millennium Commission with sponsorship from the Soap and Detergent Industry Association's Environmental Trust.

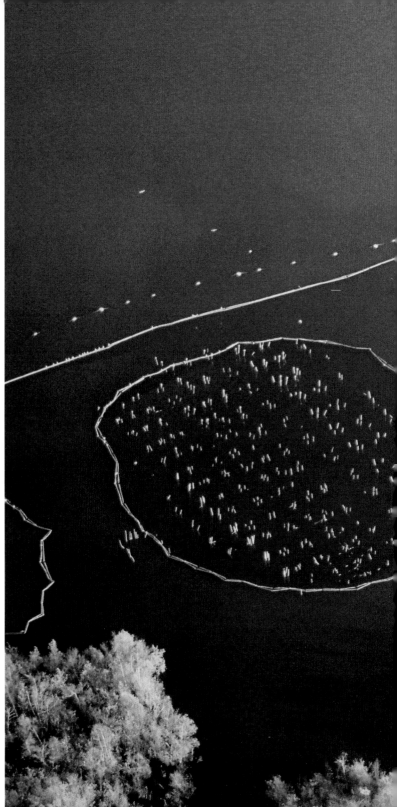

## Irstead and Barton

The hamlet of Irstead lies almost at the entrance to the broad.  The staithe leads in a straight line to the church which is a little gem.  The river bed is shallow and gravelly and known as 'Irstead Shoals'.  Turkey Broad is the bay to the left and it is in this area that much of the Clearwater programme concentrated.  Limekiln Dyke (top left) leads to Neatishead. Originally the river bypassed the broad and flowed across Catfield Fen (right), but a more efficient route, more efficient for trading sailing craft that is, was made by diverting the river into the broad.

## Alderfen Broad

Lying in the Ant valley near Irstead, landlocked Alderfen suffers the same problems of excessive enrichment by phosphates and nitrates from run-off from the surrounding land as did Barton. Some sediment has been removed by suction-dredging, and for the last ten years experiments have been carried out here to learn more about the effect of nutrient enrichment upon the fish population. A fish-proof barrier divides the broad into two. All fish except pike were removed from one half to see what effect this had on the establishment of beneficial water fleas and other small invertebrates. A similar experiment with tench was carried out in the other half. The small rectangular enclosure is an artificial fish refuge with brushes (similar to those used in Turkey Broad) providing a refuge for waterfleas and zooplankton. Perch have been introduced and their eggs attach themselves to the brushes. Alderfen is one of the broads where plant life has most declined because of water enrichment by land run off.

## How Hill looking north toward Barton Broad

The How Hill Estate was created in 1904 and since 1966 has been an environmental education centre. To the left of the river are reed beds; the small wood stands on Reedham Hill. To the right are marshes, ornamental gardens and planted woodland. The water (mid picture) is a flooded marsh with a hide for watching water birds coming in to feed at twilight. The estate has been described as the 'Broads in microcosm'. The black tower to the right of the big house is the remains of a corn grinding mill, built in 1825. The ornamental gardens (bottom left) with 'Boardman's Broad' were made by the grandson of the creator of the estate. The crop growing in lines (bottom right) is apple trees. The mill (mid picture) on the east bank was formerly known as the Skeleton Pump, being merely of wooden lattice-beam construction.

## How Hill

How Hill House commands a superb position looking over to the river and marshes beyond. How or 'haugh' means a high piece of ground surrounded by water meadows. It was built in 1904 by Norwich architect E T Boardman as his family home and has some of the features of the 'Arts and Crafts' style. He discovered the site from the river when on holiday in a wherry in 1902.

## Ludham Bridge

This bridge, replacing earlier ones and a ford, was built in the 1920s. The sharp bend approaching the bridge from downstream (near picture) causes some anxious moments when a boat bearing downstream is encountered without warning!

# THURNE

Originally the Thurne flowed north-eastwards, with its mouth on the coast somewhere between Waxham and Winterton. The river traffic in the upper reaches tends to be less than on the rest of The Broads' network because of the height restriction of the mediaeval bridge at Potter Heigham, especially during high tides or as a result of heavy rainfall. Hire Craft are required at all times to be put through by the River Pilots, and before this ruling it was not uncommon for a boat to become wedged.

## Thurne and St Benet's Level Mills

St Benet's Level Mill stands near Thurne Mouth. The mill was restored by the Crown Commission in 2001 but an electric pump drains the dykes. Both mills are typical of many Broadland drainage pumps whose towers were later 'hained' (heightened) in order to catch more wind, coinciding with the abandonment of traditional canvas sails in favour of the newer patent ones. The tower sides were extended upwards in parallel rather than having a continuation of the taper. Morse's Mill, the distinctive white one, is later (circa 1820), and was a result of the enclosure of Thurne parish. The green-roofed building in the foreground is a former First World War army hut, still in use today as holiday accommodation in an idyllic location.

## Womack Water

This small backwater of the Thurne is home to some of the most graceful and historic craft on the water. The Hunter Fleet of traditional wooden sailing boats is based here together with the winter quarters of wherry *Albion* and, occasionally, wherry *Maud*. Parishioners of Ludham may moor their boats at the staithe where, a century and more earlier, wherries would have brought cargoes of barley for the Maltings, now converted to accommodation. The village of Ludham is in the background.

## Potter Heigham

The 'Potter' arises from medieval pottery found here. This is the former Herbert Woods' Yard of excavated dykes known collectively as 'Broads Haven' and made in 1930. In addition to the numerous well-known classes of Herbert Woods' boats, many craft were built here during the Second World War including Motor Torpedo Boats (MTBs) and some of the Airborne Lifeboats, an example of which is in the Museum of The Broads at Stalham. The famous landmark tower of Broads Haven stands at the end of the boatshed complex. The riverside bungalows, which are a feature of both Potter and Thurne, line the banks on either side of the modern bridge (the former M&GN railway line).

## Candle (Kendal) Dyke and Martham Ferry

Candle Dyke leads to Heigham Sound, Hickling Broad, Meadow Dyke and Horsey Mere (top left), and Horsey Mill. Upriver of Martham Level Drainage Mill a platform swings across the river at Martham Ferry for marsh access. The flooded area upriver of the ferry is Martham Pits where clay was excavated for brick-making and more recently for bank repair. The channel across Martham Broad (top right) leads to Somerton Dyke. The broad has lost a lot of its islands because of intensive grazing by the greylag geese introduced into Norfolk in the 1930s. The proximity of the coastline demonstrates The Broads' vulnerability to invasion from the sea. This has happened several times over the centuries, the last being in 1953 when the sea broke through at Horsey Gap and thousands of acres lay under saltwater.

## Hickling Broad

Hickling is the largest of the broads with about 140 hectares of open water at present. A few years ago Hickling Broad experienced a vigorous growth of the rare waterweed Intermediate Stonewort. This was due to improved clarity of the water thereby allowing more light on to the plants. Such growth proved a problem for navigation away from the marked channel. However at present the water is fairly turbid again and plant growth is slower. Eight-storeyed Hickling corn grinding mill dominates the landscape. The staithe and Pleasure Boat Inn are centre picture. In 1917 the broad was designated as an emergency landing base for sea planes but was probably never used for this purpose.

## White holes!

The extraordinary large white patch on the entrance to Hickling Broad is a result of an abundance of water plants. In late summer the plants tend to break down and release either calcium salts or sulphur. It may be that these 'white holes' are the result of re-oxidation of the hydrogen sulphide produced by the rotting plants.

## Whiteslea Lodge

'Slea' is of Norse and Old English origin meaning a slimey, muddy stream. Originally the Lodge was a cottage on Whiteslea Broad between Heigham Sound and Hickling Broad. Lord Lucas bought it in 1912 as a base for fishing and shooting. A subsequent owner Lord Desborough raised the level of the cottage having got out of bed one morning into six inches of water! In 1946 it was bought for the Norfolk Naturalists Trust with negotiations begun by Christopher Cadbury. For much of its previous ownership Head Keeper, Jim Vincent, managed the Hickling Estate and arranged the shoots at which royalty were frequent visitors. The Lodge contains long friezes painted by the artist Roland Green who also lived on Hickling Broad. It is now a private residence.

## Horsey Mere

The orange staining in the water flowing from Waxham Cut is produced in soil which over centuries has been covered in seawater. When that land is drained there's a drop in the water table and the ochre is released. The staining is substantial in the Upper Thurne in the early summer months.

## Marietta Pallis' Grave

In the marshes on private ground near Hickling is this extraordinary piece of landscaping. It was dug out by hand in the 1950s supervised by Marietta Pallis, an ecologist and artist, who had made a special study of Broads' vegetation. It symbolises the crowned double-headed eagle, the imperial emblem of the former Greek Byzantine empire. The water surrounding the symbol was used by Miss Pallis as a swimming pool. She died in 1963 and her grave, together with that of her companion Phyllis Clarke, stands in the centre of the eagle and is marked with an iron cross.

# THE WENSUM

Saxon for 'winding', the River Wensum, sometimes called 'The Norwich River', winds its way through the city. Although it's the shortest of the Broadland rivers (4.8km from New Mills to its confluence with the Yare) it is of vital importance in connecting the city with the rest of the network. In the nineteenth century a grand scheme for creating a large harbour came to nothing, but Norwich nonetheless was a port, admittedly declining, until the 1970s. The advent of Norwich's southern bypass with its bridge over the Yare was the final act in its demise. But preceding centuries had brought timber, grain and any number of other commodities into the city. One of the first known cargoes brought here was stone from Caen in France, carried all the way by water, into Cathedral Close via a canal at what is now Pulls Ferry. This was over nine hundred years ago when the building of the cathedral began. The city walls were completed by 1343 and had twelve gates and forty towers for the defence of the city. Norwich was protected from invasion by water by two boom towers near Trowse road bridge. There a chain was stretched across the river.

## New Mills

The mills were new in 1430. A dam across the river created a head of tidal water initially to grind corn but later to pump river water up into the city. Sewage disposal was eventually dealt with by a pumping station here (1898) linking with another one at Trowse. The compressors were housed in this Victorian building. The compressed air was used in other industrial processes such as power to work the printing presses of what is now the Art School. The machinery ceased working in 1972 but still the sluices are used to control water levels.

## Aerial view of the Wensum through Norwich *Previous*

The river and the city walls together provided a medieval defence; part of the walls remain. The present-day ring road seems almost to complete a circle with the river. The oldest settled areas were near the river in the Colegate area in 'Norwich over the water'; they sit in a hollow as does the Cathedral. New developments are tucked in alongside what were former industrial buildings, and the Riverside Development (top centre) sits where ships tied up until half a century ago. The newest development of shops and housing is still in the making (centre right) on the former Nestlé site known to older Norwich residents as Caley's (chocolate factory). The Forum's distinctive horseshoe shape next to City Hall is one of the most exciting of Norwich's new buildings. The river is navigable all along the length shown here except upriver of New Mills (near centre).

## St Miles Bridge

St Miles (St Michael's) bridge is in Coslany or 'Cow Island', a low-lying part of the city. The severe floods of 1912 are marked today with a plaque showing an alarmingly high water-level, giving sense to the dragon carving and inscription on the keystone of an earlier bridge – 'When the dragon drinks, Coslany sinks'. The present bridge, now pedestrianised, dates from 1804 and is the earliest cast-iron bridge in Norwich. The river was used in the dyeing industry developed in this part of the city in the Middle Ages.

## Duke Street Bridge or Duke's Palace Bridge

There was never a bridge here when the third Duke of Norfolk chose this damp marshy site for his palace in the sixteenth century. More town house than palace, by the late seventeenth century it had been so added to that it was the largest private house in the city. Nothing now remains except the name. A cast-iron toll bridge first crossed the Wensum here in 1822. Parts of that iron bridge now provide an imposing entrance to the Castle Mall Car Park. The present concrete bridge dates from 1972 when Duke Street was widened.

## St George's (Blackfriars) Bridge

This bridge was designed in 1784 by Sir John Soane (architect locally of Shotesham Park in South Norfolk and, among other buildings, the Colonial Office of the Bank of England, and his own house in Lincolns Inn Fields, now a museum). The bridge is built of Portland Stone and has a niche where a statue was intended to sit but never did. It, in common with Foundry and Coslany Bridges, still has the spout through which a hose was inserted for uplifting river water for steam engines and fire fighting. Its alternate name derives from the Blackfriars Priory of which St Andrews Hall (the roof just in picture centre) was part. The buildings of Norwich Art School (formerly the Technical Institute) stand on either side of the road on the banks of the river. The Norwich Playhouse is across the bridge left of picture. The buildings (top) on the left-hand side of St George's Street contain flats and offices converted from one of Norwich's many shoe factories.

**Fye Bridge** *Above and Opposite*
The name may be a corruption of 'Fyvebridge' (the fifth bridge in the city) and there were quays, a ford and a staithe here long before there was a bridge. This was the area where fishing boats offloaded their catches; the street running alongside the north bank is Fishergate. The present elegant bridge dates from the 1930s. It is the site of a sixteenth-century ducking stool where 'common skolds and disreputable characters could receive the cold water cure'.

### Whitefriars Bridge *Above*

The present bridge was built in 1924 as part of a scheme to alleviate unemployment, with the river being widened at the same time. It replaced several earlier bridges and Whitefriars, (sometimes known as St Martin's), is possibly the earliest river crossing in the city. The religious order of Whitefriars (or Carmelites) established their friary in 1256 close to the bridge, on the site where Jarrolds Printing Works now stand.

*Opposite:* Looking south from Whitefriars Bridge toward the Cathedral.

**Bishop Bridge** *Above and Opposite*

Dating from around 1340, originally the bridge contained a gatehouse whose weight eventually caused structural damage and was removed around 1790. In 1923 Norwich City Council wanted the bridge widened but such was the concern that such a fine mediaeval river crossing was to be altered that the Norwich Society was founded. The Society continues to campaign for the preservation of buildings of special interest and value. At the bend in the river stands the Cow Tower, rebuilt around 1398, where at one time tolls were collected. Opposite the Cow Tower stands Petch's Corner where Petch Bros built wherries. It was in this yard around 1856 that the first Jenny Morgan wind vane was added to the wherry of the same name and ever afterwards all wind vanes have been referred to as 'Jenny Morgans.' A wherry mast marks the site.

## Foundry Bridge

A narrow bridge near the site of the now demolished Phoenix Foundry was erected in 1811 to give a good access road into the city from the growing suburb of Thorpe St Andrew. By the middle of the century a newer one had replaced it. Thorpe Station was opened in 1844 and the building of the present (third) bridge, along with the creation of Prince of Wales Road and a rebuilt railway station, had all taken place by 1890. This bridge, along with St George's and Coslany Bridges, have metal spouts (still in place) through which water could be sucked up from the river for fire fighting and steam engine boiler replenishment.

## Carrow Bridge and the Novi Sad Bridge

This is the third Carrow Bridge on the site or nearby and again the bridge building was part of an unemployment relief scheme. It was opened in 1923 by the Prince of Wales. Whilst the city was a port the single bascule opened frequently – to the great disruption of road traffic. Old paintings show how rural the location was before the advent of industrialisation; cattle were driven across the first bridge from the marshes to the Cattle Market which was in the city centre where The Mall now stands.

The Novi Sad Friendship Bridge was opened in 2001 and so called because of the twinning arrangement of the two cities. Novi Sad is in Serbia. It is a swing pedestrian bridge in a part of the city which is currently undergoing a transformation from industrial to residential use.

## Trowse Railway Swing Bridge

There has been a railway bridge across the river since 1845, before then trains going south started at Trowse. The present bridge, installed in 1986 as part of the line electrification, was temporarily welded shut in 2003 for several months because of a mechanism failure. Only rarely are steam trains seen passing over this bridge nowadays. This was *Flying Scotsman*, with a special charter, leaving Norwich on 12 September 1999.

# THE YARE

### Whitlingham Country Park *Opposite*

This picture, taken in 2001, shows the 300-acre Country Park in the making. When completed it will provide a 'lung' for Norwich, part of whose industry can be seen top right of picture. Among other features there will be a 1500 metre rowing course, and it will be possible walk the circumference of the Great Broad. The gravel workings have provided material both for Norwich's southern bypass and for the Castle Mall shopping complex. The water is divided into Whitlingham Great and Little Broads. Hart Island lies to the right of the river and railway line and the original course of the Yare was to the right of the island. With the advent of the railway the new cut was made to save wherries having to lower their masts to get under the two bridges. The railway bridge in the foreground was close to the scene of a terrible accident in 1874 when the mail train from Yarmouth crashed head on into the express from London on the then single track. Twenty-five people were killed and seventy-three injured. The Rush Cutters pub, whose car park can be seen bottom left, was used as a mortuary. The church of Thorpe St Andrew, built in, 1864 replaced an earlier one whose ruined tower stands in the churchyard.

## Whitlingham Country Park
This picture, taken three years later (2004), shows the progress made.  Gravel extraction was scheduled to finish in 2005.

## Norwich Southern Bypass

Postwick Bridge across the southern bypass (built 1990) prevented large ships reaching the city and so Norwich ceased to be a port, although the trade had been falling off for a long time. Commercial sites were then developed on the north side of the road, with the Postwick 'Park and Ride' site right of picture. Dredged spoil awaiting treatment has been deposited on the riverbank. Near the outfall on the south bank downstream of the bridge is Whitlingham Sewage Works. Upstream (far left) is the dockyard of May Gurney, Civil Engineers, who in 1940 took over the business from the firm of Hobrough who had dug part of the New Cut. As late as the 1930s Hobrough's were using redundant demasted wherries on lightering duties around the port of Norwich. It's difficult now to visualise the Water Frolics which took place in the vicinity two centuries ago.

## Woods End Bramerton *Above and Opposite*

The heavily-wooded area marks the southern edge of the wide Yare valley. This is one of the few places in The Broads network where water-skiing is permitted. Woods End pub, with its complex of red pantiled roofs, stands in the foreground and around the turn of the last century it was a favourite destination for boat trippers from Norwich. Norfolk character Billy Bluelight (real name William Cullen) on Sundays regularly used to run alongside the boat all the way to Woods End. Reputedly on the return journey as he ran he chanted 'My Name is Billy Bluelight, My age is forty-five, I hope to get to Carrow Bridge before the boat arrive'. Apparently he remained forty-five for a good many years.

**Brundall winter and summer** *Above and Opposite*

Brundall probably has more mooring places than anywhere else on The Broads' network. Boatbuilders, hire yards, riverside holiday bungalows and chalets are all within this compact area. Coldham Hall pub lies on the opposite bank, with Surlingham marshes beyond. One of many ferries across the Yare ran from here to Brundall Marsh. The pub was a favourite mooring place for wherries whilst undergoing repairs at Richard Purdy's yard.

## Wherry Graveyard Surlingham Broad

It was in the Yare Valley, and on Surlingham Broad in particular, that Dr Joyce Lambert, in collaboration with others, began taking the peat borings which led eventually to her conclusion that The Broads were man made. In the 1950s she enlisted summer holiday help from boys at the City of Norwich School and there are men now in their seventies who didn't realise at the time the significance of working with all that mud!

## Rockland Broad

Rockland Broad, also a wherry graveyard, was a favourite haunt of the nineteenth-century wildfowlers and punt gunners. Best known of all was 'Scientific' Fuller who lived in a houseboat on the broad. Eel-catcher, wildfowler, marshman, he supplemented his income by shooting rarer bird species for rich collectors. The broad has two entrances. Rockland Staithe (bottom of picture) leads to the New Inn. Ownership of the staithe has recently been transferred to the parish. To the left of the picture, and adjacent to Rockland, lies Wheatfen Broad whose natural history is one of the best documented of all the broads thanks to naturalist Ted Ellis whose home it was from 1946 until his death in 1986. Wheatfen is now in the ownership of the Ted Ellis Trust for all to enjoy.

**Buckenham** *Opposite* **and Buckenham Ferry** *Above*

The marshes, owned by the RSPB, are a haven for wildlife, especially water birds. Owls frequent the remains of Buckenham Ferry Mill (c. 1823). The last ferry ran over fifty years ago. The railway line from Reedham to Norwich borders the northern edge of the marshes which are now drained by an electric pump at the right-hand side of the mill. Beauchamp Arms is part of the complex on the opposite side of the river (the Beauchamp-Proctors were the local landowners) together with the Buckenham Sailing Club.

## Buckenham Carrs and Cantley

The winding nature of the river explains why it took so long for wind-driven trading boats to complete their journeys! At first glance this appears to be a rural landscape, but the Sugar Beet Processing Factory in the distance, with the railway and river running alongside, proves otherwise. Man-made intervention is evident also in the myriad dykes draining the marshes either side of the river, but the tree-covered areas of Buckenham Carrs are evidence of nature left to its own devices. A Broadland carr is a wet marshy area which native plants and trees have been allowed to colonise.

### *Albion* at Cantley *Above*

Wherry *Albion* at Cantley. Up until the mid 1940s this would have been a common sight. Wherries loaded beet from village staithes and brought them round by water for processing. *Albion,* having been rescued by the Norfolk Wherry Trust and given back her old name (when used as a lighter, she had been called the *Plane*), was used very briefly for beet carrying in the late 1950s and early 1960s during which time she twice sank with her load!.

### Cantley Sugar Beet Factory *Left*

The first sugar beet processing factory in the country was built here at Cantley in 1912. The distinctive sweet earthy smell which wafts over the marshes during the campaign (the processing season which runs from September to February) comes from molasses. Molasses, a byproduct, is added to the chopped beet pulp remaining after sugar extraction. The pulp then becomes a palatable animal feed. The white 'smoke' is steam from the animal feed drying process. This 1997 picture shows the coaster *Blackheath* delivering oil from Hull or Immingham into the four storage tanks on the quayside. Today all oil comes in by road. It takes only four hours to transform a root, looking somewhat like a cross between a huge turnip and a parsnip, into sugar juice. Anyone unaware of what a sugar beet looks like could consult the picturesque Cantley village sign. The huge sugar storage silos dominate the landscape.

## Reedham Ferry

The ferry carries three cars, or one lorry (in picture waiting to board), at a time. It is the only remaining chain ferry in The Broads and is operated by a diesel hydraulic winch. There are no road crossings over the Yare between Norwich's southern bypass bridge and Great Yarmouth, and the ferry operates in all weathers unless the access roads are flooded. It has been owned and operated by the Archer family, landlords of the adjacent Ferry Inn, for over fifty years.

## Reedham looking west towards Norwich

Reedham Swing bridge carries the railway line from Lowestoft to Norwich. Until fairly recently there was no radio contact between the bridge and craft on the river so even large shipping working up to Norwich and coasters taking oil to Cantley had to signal three blasts and wait for the red flag and the display board stating in how many minutes the bridge would open. Bank strengthening for flood protection is taking place at the far end of the village. In the middle distance is the Reedham Chain Ferry

## Crossing Reedham Railway Bridge

Standard 4MT engine (MT= mixed traffic) 2-6-0 no 76079 hauling 'The Easterling' train on Saturday 4 May 2002 crossing the swing bridge on a charter from Liverpool Street to Lowestoft. Charters for steam enthusiasts are still a regular feature in all parts of the country.

## Reedham looking east towards Great Yarmouth

This photograph reveals proximity of the coast – the sprawl of Great Yarmouth and the huge expanse of Breydon Water are on the skyline. The exit of the New Cut into the Yare is mid picture (right). The marshes on either side of the river have protected status.

## Haddiscoe Island

*Above:* The small picture shows some of the extensive works that have taken place along the River Yare during 2004. Raising and strengthening the riverbanks is part of a major flood defence scheme in the area.

*Opposite:* Bounded by the Yare (left), the Waveney and the New Cut, this area of marsh, with the occasional isolated house, remains one of the most remote parts of Broadland. Faden's Map of 1797 shows dwellings existing today with functional no-nonsense names such as Six Mile House, Seven Mile House and Upper Seven Mile House (since demolished); miles are measured from the Haven Bridge.

## Berney Arms Mill

Built around 1865 by Yarmouth millwright Edward Stolworthy this mill, over seventy feet tall, replaced an earlier one (1821) used for grinding clinker in the cement-making process at Thomas Berney's Reedham works. Public access is by water or via the scenic river wall path along Breydon to Yarmouth. The low building to the right houses the machinery which today drains the marshes.

## Berney, winter

The coaster *Blackheath* breaking the ice as it travels past Berney Mill in the winter of 1997.

**Berney, Yachts**
Yachts racing towards Reedham.

## The Breydon Estuary

*Above:* Breydon or 'a broadening' is precisely that – a wide stretch of water which was once a tidal estuary along which sailed Roman ships bound for Caister. The remains of the Burgh Castle Roman–Saxon fort lies on the opposite bank near the meeting of the Yare and the Waveney. The channel through Breydon has to be dredged regularly, and woe betide a boat which strays outside the marker posts to run aground and be left high and dry till the tide floats if off again. Great Yarmouth is on the skyline. Haddiscoe Island is centre picture. Raven Hall and Langley Detached Drainage Mill (detached from Langley parish near Loddon) are in the foreground (right), with Ashtree Farm, Berney Arms Mill and pub on the opposite bank.

*Opposite:* The sails have been removed from Berney mill as it undergoes complete refurbishment during 2003–2005. On the horizon, part of the new Scroby Sands windfarm is visible. This thirty-turbine windfarm was scheduled to start supplying electricity in the summer of 2004.

## Great Yarmouth

*Above:* Great Yarmouth looking south.

*Opposite:* The industry to the left of the picture (in Southtown) is in contrast to the elegant houses and Victorian splendour of the Town Hall of the South Quay. Fertiliser is still today brought in by water. The Haven lifting bridge is the last bridge across the Yare. The tall building of Haven Bridge House stands upriver. It now houses the Coastguard Service. From here sea rescues are co-ordinated, helicopters scrambled and lifeboats alerted. The River Bure joins the tidal water of Yarmouth Haven just before the Breydon Bridge. The area top left of the picture is Cobholm which was submerged in the 1953 floods.

# THE CHET

*Opposite:* The River Chet is a tributary of the Yare and is navigable only for 5.6km of its length between Loddon (Chedgrave Staithe) and its mouth. Hardley Flood about half way along its length (an SSSI), which came into being from 1940 onwards when the river embankments failed, is now in the care of the Norfolk Wildlife Trust. The river now is piled all the way to its mouth.

## Loddon

The end of navigation is here at Loddon, the villages of Loddon and Chedgrave merge. The water mill at the end of the basin contained machinery for treating seed in the 1930s. Earlier, wherries had brought grain to the mill. Starting at the staithe and across the water-meadow is a humorous sculpture trail by Mark Goldsworthy, one piece of which depicts a family trailing dropped shopping in their wake. Dropped items act as waymarks. Another example of Mark Goldsworthy's amusing work stands on the riverbank in Whitlingham Country Park.

## Hardley Cross

This unusual monument stands at the meeting of the rivers Chet and Yare. It marks the boundaries of the river jurisdictions of Norwich and Great Yarmouth. Erected in 1543 and there was an annual meeting here of the mayors of Yarmouth and Norwich to settle any boundary disputes or difficulties which had arisen in the previous twelve months. Although the practice has long been discontinued, wherry *Albion* made her first ever trip after restoration in 1949 as far as Hardley Cross with the Mayor of Yarmouth on board to be welcomed by the Lord Mayor of Norwich.

# THE WAVENEY

'Waveney' is Old English in origin and means a quaking bog or fen; the river rises in Redgrave Fen. Less than a century ago wherries worked up as far as Bungay to unload at the Staithe, but today navigation ends at Geldeston Lock. For much, but not all, of its course it serves as the county boundary between Norfolk and Suffolk. It joins the River Yare at the western end of Breydon Water and, together with the Bure, empties into the sea at Great Yarmouth. But it is linked also to Oulton Broad and Lake Lothing through Oulton Dyke and therefore exits into the sea both at Great Yarmouth and Lowestoft.

## Ellingham Mill

The river itself is off picture to the left; the mill pool can be seen both in front of and behind the mill. The gothic-windowed house on the right-hand side was the miller's home. The middle of three locks between Bungay and Geldeston lies top left of picture but is in a derelict state.

# Geldeston Lock

Also known as Shipmeadow Lock this is the first of three locks to Bungay, all of them derelict. Even in summer it's an isolated place but in winter often the marshes are flooded and then the only way out is by boat. The lock chamber can be seen in the middle ground between the present course of the river and the red roofs of the house. The footbridge crosses from Suffolk on the near side into Norfolk. 'The Locks' (centre) was originally a wherryman's pub, the original bar room still has no electricity and is lit by candles. Geldeston village lies on the higher ground.

## Beccles

Beccles was listed in the Domesday Book and was granted its charter by Elizabeth I. The land falls steeply to the river on the Suffolk side and since the west end of the church (the traditional location for the tower), is on the edge of the cliff, the church tower stands separately near the east end of the church. At one time the town's two main employers were Clowes' Caxton Printing Works and the Maltings near the railway station. When built these were reputedly the largest maltings in the world under one roof. The bright turquoise rectangle is the outdoor swimming pool sited in the picturesquely named 'Puddingmoor'. Pudding in this instance has no gastronomical connections but is possibly a corruption of 'Putta' an Anglo Saxon chief i.e. Putta's moor. There are several 'scores' or passageways leading from the high ground to the river. 'Railway Score' was next to the bridge which, from 1863, carried the Tivetshall to Beccles Waveney Valley Railway across the river (the WVR became part of the Great Eastern Railway). The line has been closed for many years and the railway bridge dismantled.

## Beccles Quay

Centre of the picture (right) and close to the river bridge stand the sawmills founded by the Darby brothers in 1846. Since this picture was taken in 1997 the buildings have been dismantled and modern houses built. The decorative chimney and the engine room feature on old photographs of wherries unloading timber. The present iron bridge was opened in 1884 and replaced at least two earlier structures. In Fen Lane (centre picture) is a complex built as a maltings, now converted to houses and to the 'Loaves and Fishes' pub. There is a slipway by the footbridge (left centre) to the right of the moored boats on the dredged out area of the quay. The children's play area (left foreground) is very popular with young holidaymakers.

## Burgh St Peter

The church (centre left) is dedicated to St Mary and not to St Peter! Its red brick tower is a Georgian curiosity being built in four stacked cubes much like a tiered wedding cake. The rest of the church is older. The Waveney River Centre provides all the boating services including fuel and groceries. The excavated marinas have pontooned moorings for about 170 craft. Oulton Dyke leading to Oulton Broad runs off to the right and the main river turns northward.

## Oulton Dyke

Where the river describes a curve towards Somerleyton, Oulton Dyke flows off to the right towards Oulton Broad, Lake Lothing and Lowestoft on the skyline. The dyke, originally a small stream, was widened and deepened, which, along with other related works (mainly the creation of Lowestoft Harbour and the New Cut), required an Act of Parliament. After much opposition from both the port of Great Yarmouth and the Dilham and North Walsham Canal who both feared their trade would diminish, the Norwich and Lowestoft Navigation Bill finally became law in 1827. The Lowestoft to Reedham Railway line runs alongside for much of the dyke's 1.5 mile length.

## Oulton Broad

This picture looking west (inland) shows Oulton Broad and Oulton Dyke. Carlton marshes (left) belong to the Suffolk Wildlife Trust. Nicholas Everitt Park (left) contains Everitt's house now a museum with a fine collection of Lowestoft porcelain. The black-roofed complex on the opposite side of the broad is a former maltings converted to flats, next to the new premises of the Waveney rush industry. Mutford Lock enables entry into Lake Lothing and the sea. It is unusual in linking two stretches of tidal water and so has to have double gates, both pointing outwards. The tide from Lake Lothing and Lowestoft is 1½ hours earlier than the tide arriving down the Waveney from Great Yarmouth. Lake Lothing begins on the seaward side ('saltside') of Mutford Lock.

## Oulton Broad and Lake Lothing

The Broads end at Mutford Lock. The coordination of lock and road bridge opening, together with liaison with the swing railway bridge, takes place in the building (centre) adjacent to the lock. The Edwardian Wherry Hotel displays its original ironwork whilst, opposite, Oulton Broad Yacht Station is unusually quiet in this winter picture. The boat centre takes passengers on cruises as far as Burgh Castle.

## Oulton Broad looking toward Lowestoft

Lowestoft harbour brings oil industry-related traffic in from the North Sea, and pleasure sailing and motor cruisers to the moorings at the new marina of the Norfolk and Suffolk Yacht Club near the harbour entrance. The Lowestoft Haven Marina is under construction (mid picture) inland of the industrial buildings on the south bank belonging to Brooke Marine and Richards' Shipbuilders. The masts (mid picture) belong to the Lowestoft Cruising Club. The white mast on the coast (centre) is at Ness Point, the most easterly place in England. The railway line from Beccles after crossing Lake Lothing merges with the line from Reedham (mid picture left) to continue into Lowestoft.

## Somerleyton

Somerleyton means 'a summer grazing place'. The wide drained marshes still afford good cattle grazing. The Lowestoft-to-Reedham railway line crosses the river via the swing bridge which opens on request. Near where the boatyard now stands a brickworks was established in 1800 – one of several in the area – and Brickfield Canal connected the works with the Waveney. Here were produced the bricks for Liverpool Street Station. Brickmaking ceased in 1939.

## Dismantled Railway Bridge, Haddiscoe

Opened in 1859 and closing one hundred years later, the East Suffolk Line ran from Beccles to Great Yarmouth (South Town) via Haddiscoe and connected via Ipswich to London. Haddiscoe had assumed an importance in the railway system, a (low level) line at right angles to the now dismantled track still runs from Lowestoft to Reedham, crossing the Waveney at Somerleyton and the Yare at Reedham. The East Suffolk (high level) line's signal box remains, as do the St Olave's swing bridge piers across the Waveney and the remains of the swing mechanism.

## Haddiscoe, The New Cut and St Olave's *Above and opposite*

Haddiscoe Bridge spans the New Cut (new in the 1830s). The New Cut was built to allow passage for trading craft from the Waveney to the Yare, avoiding the longer route via Breydon Water. The railway line, built not long afterwards, was in part responsible for the Cut's commercial failure. The rail line runs between Lowestoft and Reedham, crossing the Yare via the swing bridge. The road from Beccles to Great Yarmouth crosses both the New Cut at Haddiscoe Bridge then the Waveney over St Olave's Bridge. St Olave's, with bow-string girders, balustrades and parapets all of cast iron, was built in 1847; parts of it now have been replaced with steel. Saint Olave (or Olaf) King of Norway in the eleventh century gave his name to a nearby priory and therefore to the surrounding area. There were earlier bridges and ferries at this river crossing.

## Fritton Decoy

The water of Fritton Decoy became cut off from the river centuries ago. 'Koye' possibly of Dutch origin means a device for catching duck. Tame duck were kept in the decoy by regular feeding, these lured others into the long sausage-shaped net. With the help of a dog they were driven to its end and captured for the table; many were taken to Smithfield market.

In the 1960s a Tiger Moth with floats fitted, and in the 1990s a Catalina Flying Boat have managed to land and take off from the decoy.

## Burgh Castle

When the Romans came this whole area was part of a huge river estuary. Burgh Castle was built as a port and a shore defence fort against third-century Saxon raiders. Their town of Caister-next-Yarmouth, of which very little remains, stood on the opposite side of the estuary. The reed-covered 'rond' (the area between the embankment and the river) in the foreground would have been under water. The castle stands on the thirty foot contour. The church came several hundred years later and within its walls are Roman tiles and bricks.

## The Confluence of the Yare and The Waveney

The estuary has diminished leaving only the small area of what is now Breydon Water, but when the Romans built their fort at Burgh Castle (near the point where the two rivers now meet) they looked across a huge sheet of water to their town at Caister. The Yare and the Waveney are more strongly tidal than the River Bure because the ronds are wider. Downstream on all the rivers the ronds are salt and brackish marsh whereas further upriver they are managed for reed growing.

# Postscript

The subjects of most of the aerial pictures belonged to a particular river but included in this short section are those which cried out to be seen and which deserved a category all their own.

## The Gateway to The Broads

Visitors approaching by boat from the North Sea (and there are plenty!) enter The Broads network either via Lowestoft Harbour and Mutford Lock or here at Great Yarmouth.  The new Yarmouth Power Station dominates the South Denes (bottom right).  Privately-owned boats pass under the lifting Haven Bridge and either then join the River Bure and the Northern Broads or pass under the lifting Breydon Bridge and along Breydon Water (centre left) to the Yare or the Waveney.

## Acle Straight to Great Yarmouth

This wintry scene shows the bare bones of the landscape. Whilst the River Bure winds its way to Great Yarmouth, the A47 road (the Acle Straight) and the Norwich-to-Yarmouth (via Acle) railway line parallel each other all the way, with one bend between Acle and Yarmouth. The myriad dykes which drain Halvergate marshes run into both the Bure and Breydon Water (top of picture). The smoke from the North-Sea-gas-fired Yarmouth Power Station is on the skyline.

Less than a hundred years ago there would have been dozens of sails turning to drain these marshes, but today only the brick towers remain on most of them and the marshes are drained by electric and diesel pumps. Stracey Arms Mill (mid picture near the road and railway bend) has been restored and, although no longer working, is open to view.

## Kendal Dyke to Hickling

Kendal (Candle) Dyke (near picture) opens into Duck Broad, then Heigham Sound (with Meadow Dyke leading off abeam right to Horsey Mere) then Deep Dyke, with Swim Coots to the left, and finally into Hickling Broad. Hickling has approximately 140 hectares of open water and is the largest of the broads.

## Reed cutting

This scene could be on any Broadland marsh; it is actually at Hickling. Mechanical cutters generally have replaced scythes but there's still much handwork. Reeds have to be tied into bundles of a uniform size, combed free of litter, carried to the dyke, loaded on to a reedlighter, quanted or motored to the staithe and unloaded for collection. Sedge (for roof ridges) has to be similarly treated, except that it is cut in summer so that the reed cutter (the human variety) isn't standing inches deep in freezing water. The sight of standing reed, golden stalks and purple seed heads, in winter sunshine is unforgettable.

## Barton Regatta

Barton Regatta takes place in August each year. The dinghies in the middle of the broad are centred on the Punt Club's pontoon and on both days there are special races for Norfolk Punts. On the eastern edge of the broad one of the wherries has been pressed into service as the committee boat.

No amount of factual information can convey the atmosphere of The Broads in certain weather conditions. The following pictures attempt to do so.

## Horning

Sunshine glinting on the water at Horning Town Reach. The large craft in the middle of the river is *Southern Comfort* – a replica Mississippi Paddle Steamer. It's not exactly a traditional Broadland boat but it has become part of the scene and for many passengers it has been their introduction to The Broads.

## The Yare Valley
Seen through low early-morning mist, the smoke from the sugar beet processing factory at Cantley becomes ghostly and surreal.

## Hickling sunset
Candle Dyke, Duck Broad and Heigham Sound at twilight.

# References

*With my especial thanks to Dr Martin George PY*

ALDERTON David & Booker John, *Batsford Guide to the Industrial Archaeology of East Anglia.*

AYERS Brian, *Norwich a fine City,* (Tempus).

BLAKE, BULL, CARTWRIGHT & FITCH, *The Norfolk We Live In,* (Jarrold).

BOWSKILL Derek, *The Norfolk Broads & Fens,* (Opus).

CAMPBELL Jamie (Ed), *Hamilton's Navigations,* (Hamilton).

CLARK Roy, *Black Sailed Traders,* (David & Charles).

COCKE Sarah & HALL Lucinda, *Norwich Bridges Past & Present,* (The Norwich Society).

DUTT W A, *The Norfolk Broads,* (Methuen).

DYMOND David, *The Norfolk Landscape,* (Alastair Press).

EKWALL Eilert, *Concise Oxford Dictionary of Place Names,* (Clarendon Press).

ELLIS E A, *The Broads,* (Collins New Naturalist Series).

EWANS Martin, *Battle for The Broads,* (Terence Dalton).

FADEN, *Map of Norfolk 1797,* (Larks Press).

FRITH Anne Deed & SMITH Dorothy, *The Great Bridge of Beccles,* (Frith).

GEORGE Martin, *Land Use, Ecology and Conservation of Broadland,* (Packard).

HUTCHINSON Sheila, *The Island – Haddiscoe Island,* (Hutchinson).

LINSELL, *Hickling Broad & its Wildlife,* (Terence Dalton).

MALSTER Robert, *The Norfolk & Suffolk Broads,* (Phillimore).

MALSTER Robert, *Wherries & Waterways,* (Terence Dalton).

MEERES Frank, *Not of This World – Norfolk's Monastic Houses,* (Meeres).

MEERES Frank, *A History of Norwich.*

MOSS Brian, *The Broads,* (Harper Collins – New Naturalist Series).

NORWICH RIVER GROUP, *The Waterways of Norwich,* (Norwich Society).

OPPITZ Leslie, *Lost Railways of East Anglia,* (Countryside Books).

PEVSNER Nikolaus, *The Buildings of England* (North East Norfolk & Norwich)  Penguin.

RYE Walter, *A History of Norfolk,* (Elliot Stock).

SEYMOUR John, *The Companion Guide to East Anglia,* (Collins).

VESEY Barbara, *The Hidden Places of East Anglia,* (Travel Publishing).

WILLIAMSON Tom, *The Norfolk Broads – A Landscape History,* (Manchester University Press).

WOODS Jennifer, *Herbert Woods, A Famous Broadland Pioneer,* (Captains Locker Publications).